# MAIDSTONE AND CHATHAM TRAMWAYS

## Robert J Harley

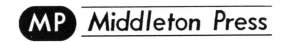

**MP** Middleton Press

Cover picture: Maidstone tramcar as described in caption 37

Cover colours: These are similar to the original livery used by the tramcars of Maidstone Corporation.

First published September 1994


ISBN 1 873793 40 5

© Middleton Press 1994

Design - Deborah Goodridge

Published by Middleton Press
            Easebourne Lane
            Midhurst
            West Sussex
            GU29 9AZ
            Tel: (0730) 813169
(From 16 April 1995 - (01730) 813169)

Printed & bound by Biddles Ltd,
            Guildford and Kings Lynn

## CONTENTS PART 1 - MAIDSTONE TRAMWAYS

## CONTENTS PART 2 - CHATHAM TRAMWAYS

## INTRODUCTION AND ACKNOWLEDGEMENTS

A favourite destination in my younger days was the town of Maidstone; the journey from my home in Eltham passed in the expectation of being allowed several rides on the trolleybuses which were the successors to the trams featured in this album. I got to know parts of the town very well and further visits, often in the company of school friends, made the area a centre of transport interest. A special treat was the granting of permission to look round Tonbridge Road depot which, although rather small by London standards, nevertheless maintained a fascination for us young enthusiasts. In the narrow confines were many relics of the tramway era and it took but little imagination to visualise trim, little four wheel tramcars bustling about the place. Sadly, all too soon, this cosy environment was shattered by an invasion of diesel buses kitted out in a rather bland pale blue livery - a poor substitute for the traditional golden ochre and cream colours which were the hallmark of the county town. After the demise of electric traction from the streets, I stayed away for some years and it was only after I met my future wife, Janet, who is a native of Maidstone, that I renewed acquaintance with the area. Our son was born in the town and later I found the time to engage in a deeper study of the transport history of this part of Kent.

My particular thanks go to all those who have helped in the preparation of this album. Photographic material of Maidstone's trams is rather sparse and to Richard Rosa, Bob Cook and David Padgham, I wish to express my gratitude. They have turned up some remarkable views which they have kindly allowed to be published for everyone to enjoy. My thanks also go to J.H.Price for his help throughout the series and to G.Croughton for supplying the tickets. I have consulted car plans drawn by P.Hammond and D.J.S.Scotney which have helped in the preparation of the rolling stock sections of this book. Finally, I owe much to Vic Mitchell, the founding father of Middleton Press, who has shown a steadfast support for the Tramway Classics albums; I would also like to thank Debby Goodridge for all her hard work in the design and production stage of each book.

# GEOGRAPHICAL SETTING

Situated in the heart of the Garden of England, Maidstone is the county town of Kent. It lies on the River Medway which was once an important means of communication. Many of the roads leading from the river valley encounter sharp gradients as they head towards the rich agricultural hinterland, much of which was formerly used for the growing of soft fruit and hops.

The town is situated in a gap in the Lower Greensand ridge of the Weald.

# HISTORICAL BACKGROUND

A settlement existed in this area during Roman times and the town then grew steadily and flourished as it was situated at an important crossing point of the River Medway on a trade route between London and the coast. The town's history has been punctuated by spells of violence; the rebellions of Wat Tyler in 1381 and Jack Cade in 1450 both disturbed the local peace. A particularly bloody incident took place on 1st June 1648, when Parliamentary forces clashed with the Royalists in five hours of hand to hand fighting in the streets. Two famous people connected with the area were Benjamin Disraeli who was first elected to Parliament as member for Maidstone in 1837, and William Hazlitt (1778-1830), the essayist, who was also a native of the town.

The South Eastern Railway arrived in 1844 at a terminus which became Maidstone West goods depot. Maidstone East station was opened by the London, Chatham and Dover Railway in 1874. The development of local industry and the expansion of housing made the idea of a local tramway system attractive, and after several false starts, the first electric line between Queen's Monument, High Street and Fountain Inn, Barming was inaugurated on 14th July 1904. The line was built to the track gauge of 3ft. 6ins./1067mm. and the fleet consisted of six four wheel, open top cars painted in a distinctive golden ochre and off-white livery. Extensions followed to Loose in October 1907 and to Tovil in January 1908; there were two depots, one on the Tonbridge Road near Barming terminus, and a smaller two track shed near the end of the Loose route. Plans were also laid for serving other parts, notably the northern half of the borough, but they came to nought; several schemes were also mooted for a direct tramway to Chatham which would have connected the two undertakings described in this album.

Receipts from the Tovil route were poor and in 1909 a single deck, one man operated demi car was put into service; the route reverted to double deck working in 1919, and the demi car was withdrawn. In the 1920s motor bus services from both the corporation and the Maidstone and District company began to play a larger role in the town's traffic. On 1st May 1928 the tramway from Queen's Monument to Barming was abandoned in favour of trolleybuses, although the access tracks to the depot were kept open for the remaining two tram services. The Tovil to Cannon line went over to motor buses in August 1929 and the last tram route to Loose finished on 11th February 1930 when car 2 closed the system. The trolleybus network was extended over the years, but that too suffered the fate of the tramways and electric traction disappeared from the streets of Maidstone in April 1967.

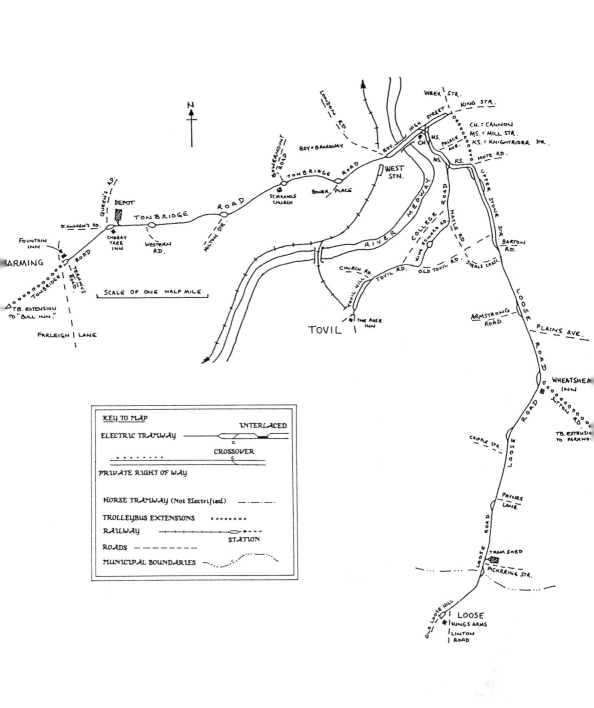

N

WEEK STR.
KING STR.
LONDON RD.
HIGH STREET
CH. = CANNON
MS. = MILL STR.
KS. = KNIGHTRIDER STR.
CN
MS.
PALACE AVE.
BDY. = BROADWAY
BDY.
MS.
KS.
MOTE RD.
SILVERMOUNT ROAD
TONBRIDGE ROAD
WEST STN.
UPPER STONE STR.
BOWER PLACE
QUEEN'S RD.
DEPOT
ST. MICHAELS CHURCH
RIVER MEDWAY
COLLEGE ROAD
HAYLE RD.
BARTON RD.
ST. ANDREW'S RD.
TONBRIDGE ROAD
KING EDWARD RD.
UPPER STONE STR.
FOUNTAIN INN
CHERRY TREE INN
WESTERN RD.
MILTON STR.
CHURCH RD.
TOVIL HILL
TOVIL RD.
OLD TOVIL RD.
NEALS CASE.
ARMSTRONG ROAD
LOOSE ROAD
PLAINS AVE.
BARMING
TONBRIDGE ROAD
TRAMS
TB. EXTENSION TO "BULL INN."
SCALE OF ONE HALF MILE
THE ROSE INN
TOVIL
WHEATSHEAF INN
SUTTON RD.
FARLEIGH LANE
TB. EXTENSION TO PARKWOOD
CRIPPLE STR.
LOOSE ROAD

KEY TO MAP
INTERLACED
ELECTRIC TRAMWAY
CROSSOVER
C
PRIVATE RIGHT OF WAY
HORSE TRAMWAY (Not Electrified)
TROLLEYBUS EXTENSIONS
RAILWAY
STATION
ROADS
MUNICIPAL BOUNDARIES

PAYNES LANE
LOOSE ROAD
TRAM SHED
PICKERING STR.
LOOSE HILL
LOOSE
KINGS ARMS
LINTON ROAD

# 1. High Street to Barming

1. At the top of the High Street car 7 waits at the terminus. In this view taken around 1906, the tram is already liberally covered with advertisements for local shops and businesses. On the right a barrel of ale is about to be shifted from a brewer's dray. (R.Rosa Coll.)

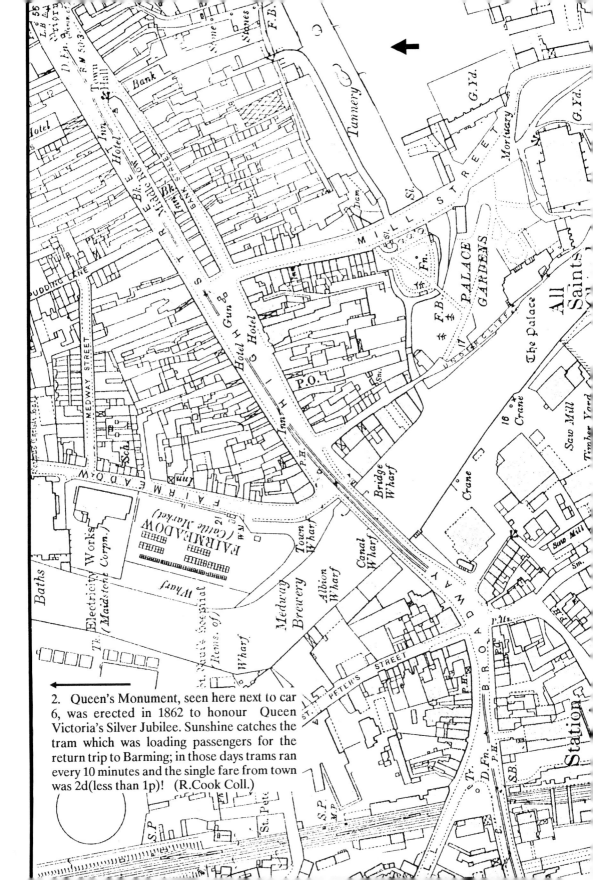

2. Queen's Monument, seen here next to car 6, was erected in 1862 to honour Queen Victoria's Silver Jubilee. Sunshine catches the tram which was loading passengers for the return trip to Barming; in those days trams ran every 10 minutes and the single fare from town was 2d(less than 1p)! (R.Cook Coll.)

3.   This postcard view of car 3 was sent on St.George's Day 1905; from the look of the tram without any adverts, the scene must date from the start of operation in the summer of 1904.  (A.J.Watkins Coll.)

# OFFICIAL TRAMWAY SERVICE.

## HIGH ST. to BARMING.

| Mon. to Sat. | | | Sunday. | |
|---|---|---|---|---|
| a m | p m | p m | p m | p m |
| 6 27 | 1 6 | 6 45 | 12 1 | 6 27 |
| 6 43 | 1 10 | 6 54 | 1217 | 6 36 |
| 6 59 | 1 19 | 7 3 | 1233 | 6 45 |
| 7 11 | 1 29 | 7 12 | 1249 | 6 54 |
| 7 23 | 1 38 | 7 21 | 1 5 | 7 3 |
| 7 35 | 1 47 | 7 30 | 1 21 | 7 12 |
| 7 47 | 1 56 | 7 39 | 1 37 | 7 21 |
| 7 59 | 2 5 | 7 48 | 1 57 | 7 30 |
| 8 11 | 2 14 | 7 57 | 2 6 | 7 39 |
| 8 23 | 2 23 | 8 6 | 2 15 | 7 48 |
| 8 35 | 2 32 | 8 15 | 2 24 | 7 57 |
| 8 47 | 2 41 | 8 24 | 2 33 | 8 6 |
| 8 59 | 2 50 | 8 33 | 2 42 | 8 15 |
| 9 11 | 2 59 | 8 42 | 2 51 | 8 24 |
| 9 23 | 3 8 | 8 51 | 3 0 | 8 33 |
| 9 36 | 3 17 | 9 0 | 3 9 | 8 42 |
| 9 47 | 3 26 | 9 9 | 3 18 | 8 51 |
| 9 59 | 3 35 | 9 18 | 3 27 | 9 0 |
| 1011 | 3 44 | 9 27 | 3 36 | 9 9 |
| 1023 | 3 53 | 9 36 | 3 45 | 9 18 |
| 1035 | 4 2 | 9 40 | 3 54 | 9 27 |
| 1047 | 4 11 | 9 45 | 4 3 | 9 36 |
| 1059 | 4 20 | 9 54 | 4 12 | 9 40 |
| 1111 | 4 29 | 10 3 | 4 21 | 9 45 |
| 1121 | 4 38 | 1012 | 4 30 | 9 50 |
| 1129 | 4 47 | 1025 | 4 39 | 10 0 |
| 1137 | 4 56 | 1035 | 4 48 | 1010 |
| 1147 | 5 5 | 11 0 | 4 57 | |
| 1156 | 5 14 | | 5 6 | |
| p m | 5 23 | | 5 15 | |
| 12 5 | 5 32 | | 5 24 | |
| 1214 | 5 41 | | 5 33 | |
| 1223 | 5 50 | | 5 42 | |
| 1232 | 6 0 | | 5 51 | |
| 1241 | 6 9 | | 6 0 | |
| 1250 | 6 18 | | 6 9 | |
| 1 0 | 6 27 | | 6 18 | |
| 1 1 | 6 36 | | | |

## BARMING to HIGH ST.

| Mon. to Sat. | | | Sunday. | |
|---|---|---|---|---|
| a m | p m | p m | a m | p m |
| 6 11 | 1 0 | 6 43 | 1145 | 5 58 |
| 6 27 | 1 9 | 6 52 | p m | 6 7 |
| 6 43 | 1 18 | 7 1 | 12 1 | 6 16 |
| 6 54 | 1 27 | 7 10 | 1217 | 6 25 |
| 7 6 | 1 36 | 7 19 | 1233 | 6 34 |
| 7 18 | 1 45 | 7 23 | 1249 | 6 43 |
| 7 30 | 1 54 | 7 37 | 1 5 | 6 52 |
| 7 42 | 2 3 | 7 46 | 1 21 | 7 1 |
| 7 54 | 2 12 | 7 55 | 1 37 | 7 10 |
| 8 6 | 2 21 | 8 4 | 1 46 | 7 19 |
| 8 18 | 2 30 | 8 13 | 1 55 | 7 28 |
| 8 30 | 2 39 | 8 22 | 2 4 | 7 37 |
| 8 32 | 2 48 | 8 31 | 2 13 | 7 46 |
| 8 54 | 2 57 | 8 40 | 2 22 | 7 55 |
| 9 6 | 3 6 | 8 49 | 2 31 | 8 4 |
| 9 18 | 3 15 | 8 58 | 2 40 | 8 13 |
| 9 30 | 3 24 | 9 7 | 2 49 | 8 22 |
| 9 42 | 3 33 | 9 16 | 2 58 | 8 31 |
| 9 54 | 3 42 | 9 25 | 3 7 | 8 40 |
| 10 6 | 3 51 | 9 34 | 3 16 | 8 49 |
| 1018 | 4 0 | 9 43 | 3 25 | 8 58 |
| 1030 | 4 9 | 9 52 | 3 34 | 9 7 |
| 1042 | 4 18 | 10 2 | 3 43 | 9 16 |
| 1054 | 4 27 | | 3 52 | |
| 11 6 | 4 36 | | 4 1 | |
| 1110 | 4 45 | | 4 10 | |
| 1118 | 4 54 | | 4 19 | |
| 1128 | 5 3 | | 4 28 | |
| 1137 | 5 12 | | 4 37 | |
| 1146 | 5 21 | | 4 46 | |
| 1155 | 5 30 | | 4 55 | |
| p m | 5 39 | | 5 4 | |
| 12 4 | 5 48 | | 5 13 | |
| 1213 | 5 56 | | 5 22 | |
| 1222 | 6 7 | | 5 31 | |
| 1231 | 6 16 | | 5 40 | |
| 1240 | 6 25 | | 5 49 | |
| 1249 | 6 34 | | | |

4. The gentleman standing to the right of car 5 is modelling a suit from the latest range offered by W.Smith's, whose wares are extolled on the tram's dash. This photo was distributed as part of a trade card togther with the motto "A Going Concern." Plenty of details can be noted on the tram, principally the trolley retriever fixed near the fleet number and the powerful headlight on the canopy above the motorman. In an age still wedded to the candle and the gaslamp, the new electric marvels running along the streets at night must have truly seemed "galleons of light." (R.Cook Coll.)

High Street, Maidstone. No. 2.

Cooper's Series
Co. Maidstone.

5. The terminus has now acquired a waiting shelter and the trams have been fitted with indicator boxes. We are looking down the High Street towards the Medway. (R.Rosa Coll.)

7. The Tovil route opened in January 1908 and in 1910 the service was cut back to start at the Cannon. Car 11 is pictured between these dates in the company of the water car which was supplied to the corporation in 1908. (R.Rosa Coll.)

6. The Carlton Cafe Oriental Tea Room and the fine, if somewhat overblown, edifice of the London, County and Westminster Bank set the scene as a tram sets off past the cabs. The latter form of transport catered almost exclusively for the well-to-do, most ordinary folk took the tram. (D.C.Padgham Coll.)

Official Opening
OF THE
Maidstone Tramway,
July 14th, 1904.

8. Further along the High Street outside the Town Hall, we witness the opening ceremony of the tramways; four of the original six trams are in sight. No doubt the other two cars are waiting at the Barming end to transport excited villagers into town. Contemporary reports indicate that at least one tram on opening day was found to contain 80 passengers, well over the legal limit! (D.C.Padgham Coll.)

10. High Street in 1994 is the scene where queues of vehicles emitting petrol and diesel fumes are commonplace. The contrast with this view of a summer's day in the first decade of the twentieth century, could not be greater. The tramcar symbolises a gentler, less hurried, and more environmentally friendly approach to life. (J.H.Price Coll.)

9. Looking very smart in "as delivered" condition, car 5 halts to pick up a passenger. (R.Cook Coll.)

11. From a vantage point above ground level we get a bird's eye view up the High Street in the direction of Queen's Monument. A well laden tram has just passed the carriers' wagons parked next to the Cannon. (R.Rosa Coll.)

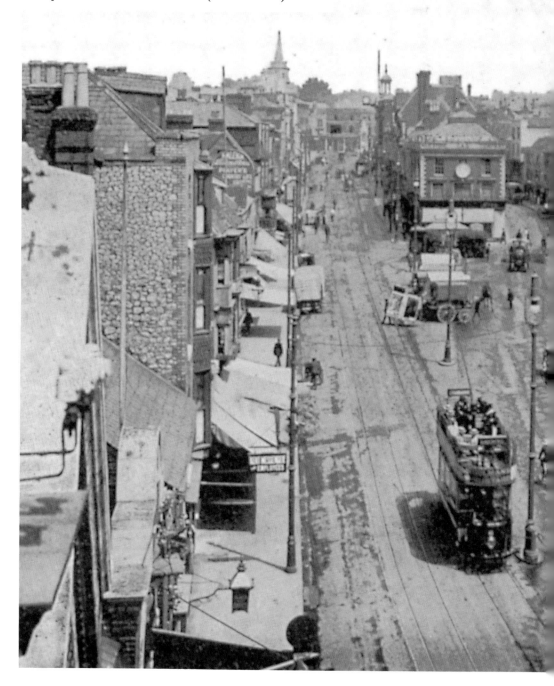

BAZAAR

27044

12. We return to terra firma in time to catch sight of car 1 outbound to Barming. There is plenty of commercial activity and the number of vehicles suggests the photo was taken on market day; local trade depended greatly on carriers transporting goods and produce to and from outlying areas. (R.J.Harley Coll.)

13. An ominous sign for the future is the notice of the Maidstone Motor Garage. However, in this 1909 High Street scene, the pace of life was

14. Car 4 has just crossed the bridge over the Medway, situated behind the photographer. The tram is approaching the original single track which was later doubled in 1908. (J.H.Price Coll.)

still geared to the horse and cart. (R.Rosa Coll.)

2. High Street, Maidstone

# OFFICIAL TRAMWAY SERVICE.

## CANNON to LOOSE.

| Mon. to Fri. | | Saturday. | | Sunday |
|---|---|---|---|---|
| a m | p m | a m | p m | p m | p m |

| a m | p m | a m | p m | p m | p m |
|---|---|---|---|---|---|
| 5 54 | 4 45 | 5 54 | 4 10 | 1220 | 7 50 |
| 6 13 | 5 0 | 6 13 | 4 20 | 1 0 | 8 0 |
| 6 32 | 5 10 | 6 32 | 4 30 | 1 40 | 8 10 |
| 6 51 | 5 20 | 6 51 | 4 40 | 2 0 | 8 20 |
| 7 10 | 5 30 | 7 10 | 4 50 | 2 10 | 8 30 |
| 7 30 | 5 40 | 7 30 | 5 0 | 2 20 | 8 40 |
| 7 50 | 5 50 | 7 50 | 5 10 | 2 30 | 8 50 |
| 8 10 | 6 0 | 8 10 | 5 20 | 2 40 | 9 0 |
| 8 30 | 6 10 | 8 30 | 5 30 | 2 50 | 9 10 |
| 8 50 | 6 20 | 8 50 | 5 40 | 3 0 | 9 20 |
| 9 10 | 6 30 | 9 10 | 5 50 | 3 10 | 9 30 |
| 9 35 | 6 40 | 35 | 6 0 | 3 20 | |
| 10 06 | 6 50 | 10 0 | 6 10 | 3 30 | |
| 1020 | 7 0 | 1020 | 6 20 | 3 40 | |
| 1040 | 7 10 | 1040 | 6 30 | 3 50 | |
| 11 0 | 7 20 | 11 0 | 6 40 | 4 0 | |
| 1120 | 7 30 | 1120 | 6 50 | 4 10 | |
| 1140 | 7 40 | 1140 | 7 0 | 4 20 | |
| p m | 7 50 | 12 0 | 7 10 | 4 30 | |
| 12 0 | 8 10 | 1220 | 7 20 | 4 40 | |
| 1220 | 8 20 | 1240 | 7 40 | 4 50 | |
| 1240 | 8 30 | 1250 | 7 50 | 5 0 | |
| 1250 | 8 45 | 1 4 | 8 0 | 5 10 | |
| 1 4 | 9 0 | 1 20 | 8 10 | 5 20 | |
| 1 20 | 9 15 | 1 3_ | 8 20 | 5 30 | |
| 1 30 | 9 30 | 1 40 | 8 30 | 5 40 | |
| 1 40 | 9 45 | 2 0 | 8 40 | 5 50 | |
| 2 1 | 1010 | 2 10 | 8 50 | 6 0 | |
| 2 15 | 1020 | 2 30 | 9 0 | 6 10 | |
| 2 30 | | 2 40 | 9 10 | 6 20 | |
| 2 45 | | 2 50 | 9 20 | 6 30 | |
| 3 0 | | 3 0 | 9 30 | 6 40 | |
| 3 15 | | 3 10 | 9 40 | 6 50 | |
| 3 30 | | 3 20 | 9 50 | 7 0 | |
| 3 45 | | 3 30 | 1010 | 7 10 | |
| 4 0 | | 3 40 | 1020 | 7 20 | |
| 4 15 | | 3 50 | | 7 30 | |
| 4 30 | | 4 0 | | 7 40 | |

## LOOSE to CANNON.

| Mon. to Fri. | | Saturday. | | Sunday. | |
|---|---|---|---|---|---|
| a m | p m | a m | p m | p m | p m |

| a m | p m | a m | p m | p m | p m |
|---|---|---|---|---|---|
| 6 13 | 4 50 | 6 13 | 4 0 | 1240 | 8 20 |
| 6 32 | 5 5 | 6 32 | 4 10 | 1 20 | 8 30 |
| 6 51 | 5 20 | 6 51 | 4 20 | 2 0 | 8 40 |
| 7 10 | 5 30 | 7 10 | 4 30 | 2 20 | 8 50 |
| 7 30 | 5 40 | 7 30 | 4 40 | 2 30 | 9 0 |
| 7 50 | 5 50 | 7 50 | 4 50 | 2 40 | 9 10 |
| 8 10 | 6 0 | 8 10 | 5 0 | 2 50 | 9 20 |
| 8 21 | 6 10 | 8 21 | 5 10 | 3 0 | 9 30 |
| 8 30 | 6 20 | 8 30 | 5 20 | 3 10 | 9 40 |
| 8 48 | 6 30 | 8 48 | 5 30 | 3 20 | 9 50 |
| 9 10 | 6 40 | 9 10 | 5 40 | 3 30 | |
| 9 30 | 6 50 | 9 30 | 5 50 | 3 40 | |
| 10 0 | 7 0 | 10 0 | 6 0 | 3 50 | |
| 1020 | 7 10 | 1020 | 6 10 | 4 0 | |
| 1040 | 7 20 | 1040 | 6 20 | 4 10 | |
| 11 0 | 7 30 | 11 0 | 6 30 | 4 20 | |
| 1120 | 7 50 | 1120 | 6 40 | 4 30 | |
| 1140 | 8 0 | 1140 | 6 50 | 4 40 | |
| p m | 8 10 | p m | 7 0 | 5 0 | |
| 12 0 | 8 30 | 12 0 | 7 10 | 5 10 | |
| 1220 | 8 40 | 1220 | 7 20 | 5 20 | |
| 1230 | 8 50 | 1230 | 7 30 | 6 30 | |
| 1240 | 9 5 | 1240 | 7 40 | 6 40 | |
| 1 0 | 9 20 | 1 0 | 7 50 | 6 50 | |
| 1 10 | 9 30 | 1 10 | 8 0 | 7 0 | |
| 1 20 | 9 46 | 1 20 | 8 10 | 7 10 | |
| 1 41 | 10 2 | 1 41 | 8 20 | 7 20 | |
| 1 53 | 1040 | 1 53 | 8 30 | 7 30 | |
| 2 0 | | 2 0 | 8 40 | 7 40 | |
| 2 19 | | 2 20 | 8 50 | 7 50 | |
| 2 35 | | 2 30 | 9 0 | 8 0 | |
| 2 51 | | 2 40 | 9 10 | 8 10 | |
| 3 6 | | 2 50 | 9 20 | | |
| 3 21 | | 3 0 | 9 30 | | |
| 3 36 | | 3 10 | 9 40 | | |
| 3 50 | | 3 20 | 9 50 | | |
| 4 5 | | 3 30 | 10 0 | | |
| 4 20 | | 3 40 | 1010 | | |
| 4 35 | | 3 50 | 1040 | | |

15. The West station was, for a short while in 1909, the terminus for the Loose service. Local children crowd round the tram, no doubt hoping to catch the photographer's eye. One wonders what sort of gastronomic experience it was to consume the product so boldly advertised on the front of car 11! (R.Rosa Coll.)

16. Strict timetabling was enforced on the single track sections to avoid the danger and embarrassment of two trams meeting head-on. This view of Tonbridge Road near Bower Place shows car 5 beginning the descent to Broadway and the West station.
(R.Rosa Coll.)

17. In the distance two trams pass on the loop opposite Bowermount Road. Of particular tramway interest is the traction standard to the right of the picture; these reflected municipal pride and were topped with fluted urn finials. Many of the finials survived into the trolleybus era and were later preserved to adorn the poles at the National Tramway Museum in Crich, Derbyshire. (R.J.Harley Coll.)

→

18. A well known view, taken just after service started in 1904, depicts car 3 passing a couple of young cyclists. In the background is the tower of St.Michael's Church which was built in 1876. (R.J.Harley Coll.)

→

19. Nearing the terminus, we reach the gates of the depot in Tonbridge Road, seen here in trolleybus days. The transport offices are housed in the building with the fine entrance porch. (R.Cook Coll.)

20. In the depot yard preparations are made before a car takes up service. Note the conductor with his ticket rack and the sombre motorman in the traditional motorman's coat lined with sparkling brass buttons, each one embossed with the Maidstone coat of arms. (R.J.Harley Coll.)

21. A couple of dapper young men are pictured with the first trams of the fleet under cover in the original depot building. An extension with two further roads was added to the left of car 1 in 1908. (R.Cook Coll.)

22. Eighty years after the previous view and the depot is still easily recognised. The survival of some tram rails after the World War II scrap metal drives is remarkable. (R.J.Harley)

23. The headlight mask and the presence of the conductress indicate that the First World War is still raging. The town received an air raid warning in June 1917, which probably justified the blackout restrictions on the tram. Car 7 stands on the western side of the depot and, in spite of wartime shortages, still looks well turned out. (R.Cook Coll.)

24. Some of the pointwork still remains on the depot forecourt surrounded by the typical granite setts or "cobbles" of the tramway period. (R.J.Harley)

COULTER'S
CROCKERY IS THE STRONGEST
16, LOWER STONE STREET

# OFFICIAL TRAMWAY SERVICE.

## TOVIL to CANNON.

| Mon. to Fri. | | Saturday | | Sunday |
|---|---|---|---|---|
| a m | p m | a m | p m | p m |
| 6 35 | 8 20 | 6 35 | 4 50 | 2 15 |
| 6 55 | 8 40 | 6 55 | 5 0 | 2 35 |
| 7 15 | 9 0 | 7 15 | 5 10 | 2 55 |
| 7 35 | 9 20 | 7 35 | 5 20 | 3 15 |
| 7 55 | 9 40 | 7 55 | 5 30 | 3 35 |
| 8 15 | 10 0 | 8 15 | 5 40 | 3 55 |
| 8 35 | 10 20 | 8 35 | 5 50 | 4 15 |
| 8 55 | | 8 55 | 6 0 | 4 35 |
| 9 15 | | 9 15 | 6 10 | 4 55 |
| 9 35 | | 9 35 | 6 20 | 5 15 |
| 9 55 | | 9 55 | 6 30 | 5 35 |
| 10 15 | | 1015 | 6 40 | 5 55 |
| 10 35 | | 1035 | 6 50 | 6 15 |
| 10 55 | | 1055 | 7 0 | 6 35 |
| 11 15 | | 1115 | 7 10 | 6 55 |
| 11 35 | | 1135 | 7 20 | 7 15 |
| 11 55 | | 1155 | 7 30 | 7 35 |
| p m | | p m | 7 40 | 7 55 |
| 12 15 | | 1215 | 7 50 | 8 15 |
| 12 37 | | 1237 | 8 0 | 8 35 |
| 1 3 | | 1 3 | 8 10 | 8 55 |
| 1 13 | | 1 13 | 8 20 | 9 15 |
| 1 22 | | 1 22 | 8 30 | 9 35 |
| 1 40 | | 1 31 | 8 40 | |
| 2 0 | | 1 40 | 8 50 | |
| 2 20 | | 1 50 | 9 0 | |
| 2 40 | | 2 0 | 9 10 | |
| 3 0 | | 2 10 | 9 20 | |
| 3 20 | | 2 20 | 9 30 | |
| 3 40 | | 2 30 | 9 40 | |
| 4 0 | | 2 40 | 10 0 | |
| 4 20 | | 2 50 | 1020 | |
| 4 40 | | 3 0 | | |
| 5 0 | | 3 10 | | |
| 5 20 | | 3 20 | | |
| 5 40 | | 3 30 | | |
| 6 0 | | 3 40 | | |
| 6 20 | | 3 50 | | |
| 6 40 | | 4 0 | | |
| 7 0 | | 4 10 | | |
| 7 20 | | 4 20 | | |
| 7 40 | | 4 30 | | |
| 8 0 | | 4 40 | | |

## CANNON to TOVIL.

| Mon. to Fri. | | Saturday | | Sunday |
|---|---|---|---|---|
| a m | p m | a m | p m | p m |
| 6 25 | 8 10 | 6 25 | 4 40 | 2 5 |
| 6 45 | 8 30 | 6 45 | 4 50 | 2 25 |
| 7 5 | 8 50 | 7 5 | 5 0 | 2 45 |
| 7 25 | 9 10 | 7 25 | 5 10 | 3 5 |
| 7 45 | 9 30 | 7 45 | 5 20 | 3 25 |
| 8 5 | 9 50 | 8 5 | 5 30 | 3 45 |
| 8 25 | 1010 | 8 25 | 5 40 | 4 5 |
| 8 45 | | 8 45 | 5 50 | 4 25 |
| 9 5 | | 9 | 6 0 | 4 45 |
| 9 25 | | 9 25 | 6 10 | 5 5 |
| 9 45 | | 9 45 | 6 20 | 5 25 |
| 10 5 | | 10 5 | 6 30 | 5 45 |
| 1025 | | 1025 | 6 40 | 6 5 |
| 1045 | | 1045 | 6 50 | 6 25 |
| 11 5 | | 11 5 | 7 0 | 6 45 |
| 1125 | | 112 | 7 10 | 7 5 |
| 1145 | | 1145 | 7 20 | 7 25 |
| p m | | p m | 7 30 | 7 45 |
| 12 5 | | 12 5 | 7 40 | 8 5 |
| 1227 | | 1227 | 7 50 | 8 25 |
| 1250 | | 1250 | 8 0 | 8 45 |
| 1 4 | | 1 4 | 8 10 | 9 5 |
| 1 13 | | 1 13 | 8 20 | 9 25 |
| 1 31 | | 1 23 | 8 30 | |
| 1 50 | | 1 31 | 8 40 | |
| 2 10 | | 1 40 | 8 50 | |
| 2 30 | | 1 50 | 9 0 | |
| 2 50 | | 2 0 | 9 10 | |
| 3 10 | | 2 10 | 9 20 | |
| 3 30 | | 2 20 | 9 30 | |
| 3 50 | | 2 30 | 9 50 | |
| 4 10 | | 2 40 | 1010 | |
| 4 30 | | 2 50 | | |
| 4 50 | | 3 0 | | |
| 5 10 | | 3 10 | | |
| 5 30 | | 3 20 | | |
| 5 50 | | 3 30 | | |
| 6 10 | | 3 40 | | |
| 6 30 | | 3 50 | | |
| 6 50 | | 4 0 | | |
| 7 10 | | 4 10 | | |
| 7 30 | | 4 20 | | |
| 7 50 | | 4 30 | | |

←

25. Inside the building car 9 is positioned over one of the inspection pits which gave access for maintenance staff to the underside of the tramcar. Athough the trolley retrievers had been given up some years previously, the catch fitting is still on the dash. (R.Cook Coll.)

26. In the period 1928-30, the eastern side of the depot was converted for use by the new trolleybuses. As can be seen, this entailed filling in the former tramway maintenance pits; the other half of the depot retained all the equipment needed for the remaining tramcars. (R.Cook Coll.)

LY5711

1d

| FROM | | FROM |
|---|---|---|
| Tovil to High St | | Barming to St. Mich. Ch |
| Lense to Wheat- Sheaf | | Western Lense to Barming |
| Swan to Old Tovil Rd | | Milton Street to High St |
| Wheat Sheaf to S.E. Sta | | S.E. St. to Wheat Sheaf |
| High St. to Milton St | | Old Tovil Rd to Swan |
| Bower Street to Western Road | | Wheat- Sheaf to Loose |
| St. Mich. Church to Barming | | High St. to Tovil |

Maidstone Corporation Tramways.

The ticket is only subject to the Bye Laws of the Corporation, must be produced for inspection when required, or given up on demand, and must be retained in the section over which the Passenger is entitled to travel.

Williamson, Printer, Ashton

Tonbridge Road, Maidstone.

27. The passing loop outside the depot was also situated opposite the Cherry Tree Inn. Car 3 halts for a sister car which has ascended Tonbridge Road from town. (R.J.Harley Coll.)

28. Some parts of Tonbridge Road were little more than a country lane when the first tram tracks were laid, and evidence of road widening can be spotted in this early view. (R.Cook Coll.)

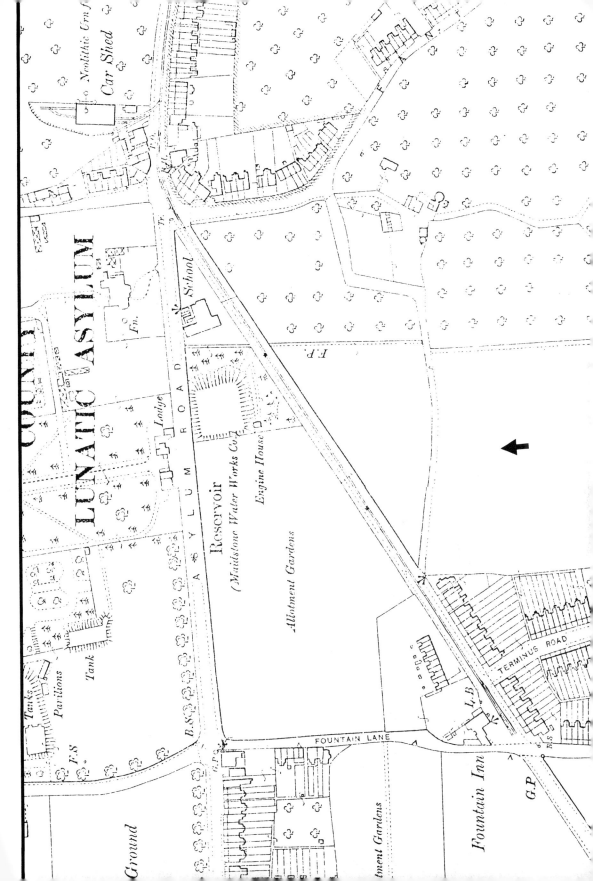

29. We can guess that it was a hot day, so the water car was needed to lay the dust here at journey's end outside the Fountain Inn. Whether the lack of crew indicates that they were inside the hostelry slaking their thirst and imbibing the products of Messrs. Style and Winch, we shall never know! (R.Cook Coll.)

30. George Gundry visited Maidstone in 1922 and snapped car 2 at the Fountain. (G.L.Gundry)

| Ra | 2295 | |
|---|---|---|
| FROM | 1d. | FROM |
| Tovil to High St. | | Barming to St. Mich. Ch. |
| Loose to Wheat-sheaf | | Western Road to Bower St. |
| Swan to Old Tovil Rd | | Milton Street to High St. |
| Wheat-sheaf to B. E. Stn. | | S. E. Stn. to Wheat-sheaf |
| High St. Milton Street | | Old Tovil Rd. to Swan |
| Bower Street to Western Road | | Wheat-shed to Loose |
| St.Mich. Church to Barming | | High St. to Tovil |
| Bell Punch Company, London | | |

31. Photos of the one man operated demi car are rare, so we are particularly fortunate to have a chance to observe the car at Barming. As the destination blind and side board suggest, the car's usual stamping ground was the Tovil to Cannon service. (R.Cook Coll.)

32. Electric traction on the streets of Maidstone was perpetuated in the form of the trolleybus, here no. 66 basks in the autumn sunshine of 1964 opposite the aptly named Terminus Road, Barming. Even after the trolleybus service was extended further down the road to the Bull Inn, vehicles regularly worked to the old tramway terminus at the Fountain. (R.J.Harley)

# 2. Cannon to Tovil

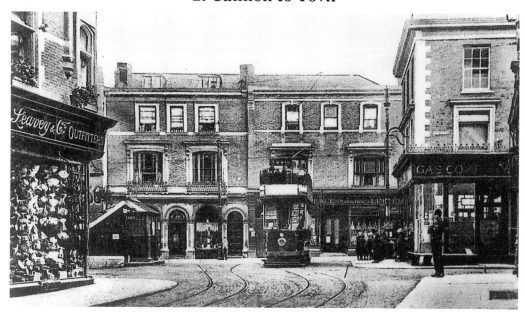

33. All aboard for Tovil. Car 8 waits at the junction of Mill Street and High Street for the short run along College Road, King Edward Road and down Tovil Hill to the paper mill. The route was normally worked as a shuttle service with a single tram, the fare at this time was just one old penny! (R.J.Harley Coll.)

34. The flags are out for Cricket Week; the conductor turns the pole, the motorman checks his waybill and two lads make their way to a seat on the top deck in this fine late 1920s study of car 11 at the Cannon. (H.A.Whitcombe)

35. Car 16 coasts down Tovil Hill shortly before the tramway was replaced by motor buses. The village of Tovil was one of the smallest places in Britain to be served by both a branch railway and an electric tramway. (R.Cook Coll.)

36. In this picture of Tovil Hill the double track leading from the terminal stub can clearly be seen. When the line was worked by car 18, the motorman cum conductor would start the tram rolling from the terminus and then, as the car slowly ground up the hill, he would leave his post to collect the fares. This early example of "driverless operation" was frowned upon by the authorities, but there are no accounts of any accidents on the Tovil route. (R.J.Harley Coll.)

37. The conductor in his white topped summer hat grasps the trolley rope ready for the reversal outside the paper mill at Tovil. Note the lack of passengers, not an unusual occurrence on this line, and the curtains in the lower saloon which add a touch of domesticity to the tram. (H.A.Whitcombe)

38. The photographer has his back to the Rose public house as his lens catches the crew of car 11 having a quick "light up" at the terminus. Notice the tree trunk on the logging cart with the horse standing patiently by. (R.Rosa Coll.)

# 3. Cannon to Loose

39. At the Cannon an unidentified car of the 1-7 batch waits for the conductor to signal departure for Loose (pronounced "looz"). (H.A.Whitcombe)

40. Out on the Loose Road near the Wheatsheaf Inn, car 17 waits at the loop for the tram from town. Although the road is wide enough, nothing has been done to improve the track layout, which still hugs the eastern side of the carriageway. (J.H.Price Coll.)

41. Loose tram shed by Pickering Street provided overnight accommodation for the first inbound Loose to Cannon car of the day. The building had a maximum capacity of four trams and it survived as a vehicle store throughout the trolleybus years. It is seen here in November 1963. (R.J.Harley Coll.)

42. Loose village lies in the valley below the tram terminus which was situated on Old Loose Hill just by the Kings Arms. The trams gave many inhabitants of Maidstone a chance to get out into the countryside and enjoy the hop gardens, streams, meadows and orchards of the Kentish Weald. (R.Rosa Coll.)

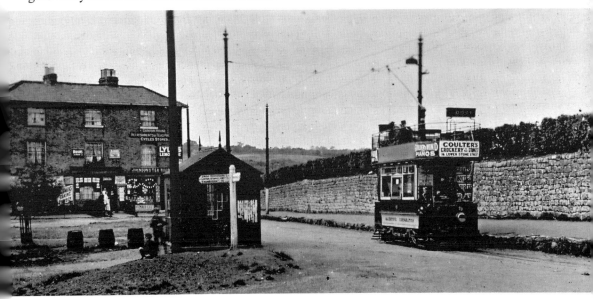

43. The sun shines brightly on a setting from long ago. In the middle of the picture by the signpost is the waiting room for passengers who had struggled up Loose Hill just to see the car disappear round the corner! The conductor of the last cheap fares car before 8 am would often hold the tram a minute or so to wait for stragglers who needed the benefit of the concessionary workman's fare. (R.J.Harley Coll.)

44. The postcard photographer has nipped round the back of the next arrival at the terminus, which turns out to be car 9. We are looking away from Loose towards town. The state of local dentistry is illustrated by the advertising blurb for Ford's "Humane" teeth extraction system..."it doesn't hurt a bit"..! (R.Cook Coll.)

45. The cylindrical object on the pavement to the left of the tram is not a post box but one of the distinctive Maidstone feeder pillars which contained circuit breaker switches for the traction current. They were positioned every half mile along the tramway and many remained after abandonment to serve the trolleybuses. (G.L.Gundry)

46. The date is 16th October 1907 and the inaugural car from Loose to the High Street is posed for the historic occasion. Most of the journey from town passed along what was then little more than a country lane bordered by tall trees and hedgerows. The track was laid at the side of the road and children on the top deck often used to amuse themselves by watching the leaves of overhanging branches sweep the hats from the heads of their fellow travellers. A cheer would then go up and many an unfortunate gentleman would have to descend quickly to retrieve his straw boater; ladies, of course, secured their head gear with a hat pin! The tram would then coast to a halt as the motorman waited, with a courtesy common at that time, for the pasenger to reboard. (R.Rosa Coll.)

47. The terminal arrangements at Loose are simple yet comprehensive. There is a clock fixed to the traction standard on the left which shows the time of the next departure. The waiting room is to the right of the picture near a siding for any extra trams; finally, an electric light is attached above the wires to help passengers and crew at night. (A.J.Watkins Coll.)

48. This scene is still recognisable from the last photo as trolleybus 64 slows for the turn in front of the Kings Arms in October 1964. (R.J.Harley)

# 4. Rolling Stock

Maidstone trams were painted in an attractive livery of golden ochre and off white which was retained for the replacing buses and trolleybuses. As some cars got older and the varnish weathered, so the hue changed to brown with a khaki tinge. Trucks and undergear were painted red oxide and the title of the undertaking was picked out on the rocker panel in gold letters shaded red; the coat of arms of the town was placed centrally on the waist panel of each tram.

**CARS 1-7.** These were traditional four wheel, open top trams which arrived in May 1904 with car 7 following in February 1907. Each car seated 22 inside and 26 on the top deck; the benches in the lower saloon were covered with red carpet and maroon curtains were placed at the windows. Originally a fixed head trolley was fitted which was connected via the trolley rope to a trolley retriever attached to the dash of the tram. At every reversal it was the conductor's job to lift off the retriever and fix it to the opposite end of the car ready for departure. In 1907-8 a normal swivel head trolley replaced the fixed head variety and the spring loaded trolley retrievers were later given up. Other alterations included the repositioning of the headlamp from the canopy to the dash and a roller blind destination box above the upper deck handrails. The destination box was subsequently moved after 1918 to the edge of the canopy above the motorman. Route boards were inserted into brackets fitted under the centre saloon windows. Each tram had an overall length of 27ft. 8ins. and rode on a 6ft. wheelbase Brill 21E truck. Withdrawal took place in 1929-30.

**CARS 8-17.** These trams were supplied in

1907, they were shorter than cars 1-7, being constructed to an overall length of 24ft. 8ins.. They were of a very similar design to the first batch of trams and they retained the direct quarter-turn stairs which were unusual for this style of tramcar. Seating was for 18 inside and 22 on the top deck. The original upper deck mounted indicator boxes were repositioned to a location under the canopy, as described on cars 1-7. Car 14 was sold to Chatham in 1928 and the rest were withdrawn in 1929-30.

CAR 18. This was a one man operated demi car supplied in 1909 for the Tovil route. Transverse seats were fitted in the saloon for 15 people and a bench by the driver seated a further two persons. The car was delivered with a trolley retriever. By 1919 passenger levels on the Tovil service had improved and a double deck car was drafted in to take over from car 18. The demi car was then withdrawn from service although it did emerge to help out in emergencies. Around 1926 it was permanently confined to the depot and it was disposed of in 1928 only to be rediscovered in 1970 in use as a holiday caravan. The body of the car is now at the Dover Transport Museum awaiting restoration.

WATER CAR. This formidable vehicle, known to the staff as "Dreadnought", was delivered in 1908. Its main functions were to sweep the tracks, to keep the rail grooves free of detritus, and to water the road in hot weather. The title Maidstone Corporation appeared in gold lettering on the water tank sides and the car was painted in an all over golden ochre livery similar to the passenger cars. It was last used in 1921 and was scrapped around 1925.

49. The official view taken at the Electric Railway & Tramway Carriage Works Ltd. of Preston, Lancashire of Car 6. The pristine state of the tram is a tribute to the craftmanship of the builders. (ERTCW. R.Cook Coll.)

50. A detailed shot of the platform of the car pictured previously, depicts the alterations to the tram at about the time of World War I. Advertising has appeared on the steps and top deck decency board, the notice WAIT UNTIL THE CAR STOPS has been pasted to the bulkhead window, the headlamp has been moved to the dash and the platform lattice gates have disappeared. (R.Rosa Coll.)

51. Modelmakers can glean much information from this end on view of car 4. Notice that one of the lifeguard slats is damaged and that the headlamp is partially masked to conform with blackout regulations.  (R.Cook Coll.)

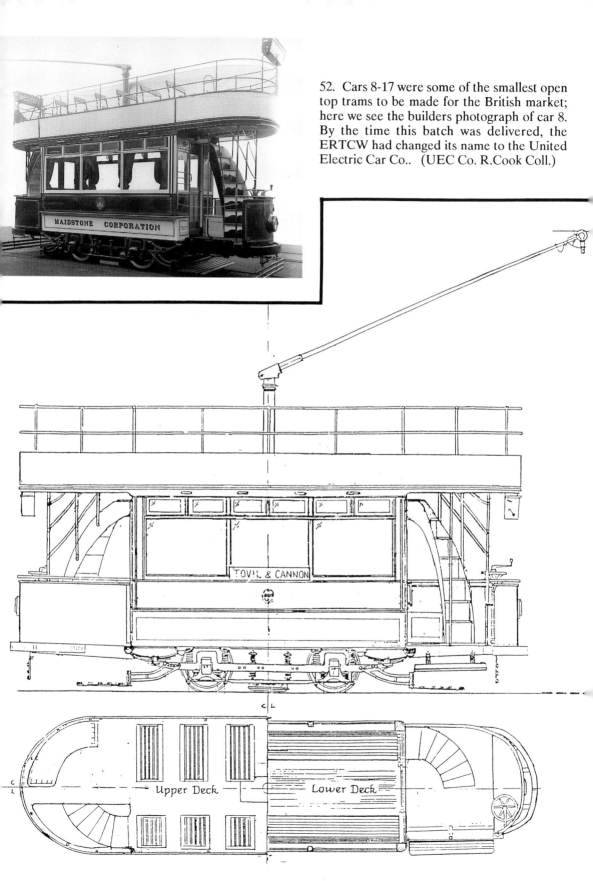

52. Cars 8-17 were some of the smallest open top trams to be made for the British market; here we see the builders photograph of car 8. By the time this batch was delivered, the ERTCW had changed its name to the United Electric Car Co.. (UEC Co. R.Cook Coll.)

MAIDSTONE CORPORATION

TOVIL & CANNON

Upper Deck — Lower Deck

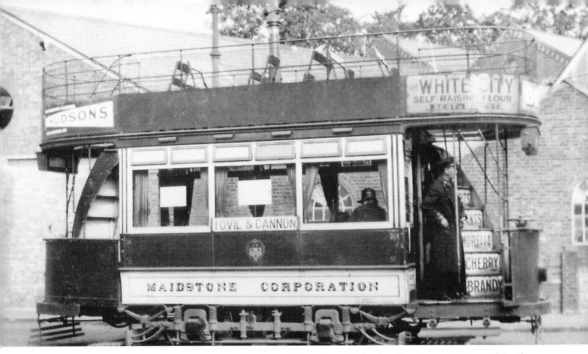

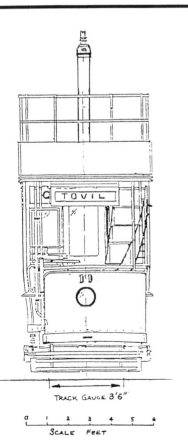

TRACK GAUGE 3'6"

```
0   1   2   3   4   5   6
    SCALE   FEET
```

53. Car 11 is in final condition with the indicator box placed above the motorman's platform. (H.A.Whitcombe)

54. In their twilight years many British trams had retirement careers as garden sheds or even residences by the seaside. Car 14 languishes in a Kentish orchard; the long bench seat and the wooden panelling still survive in this photograph taken some 34 years after the car left the rails. (R.Cook)

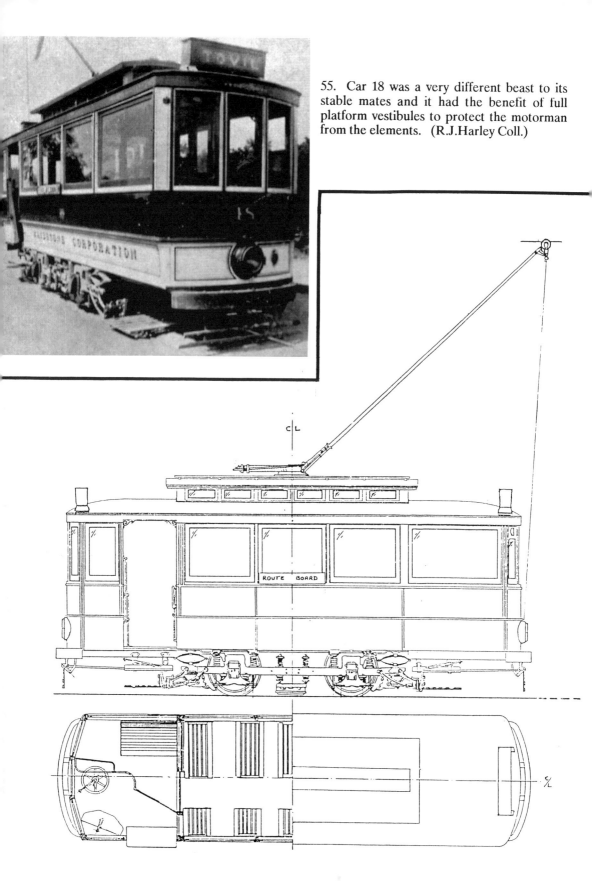

55. Car 18 was a very different beast to its stable mates and it had the benefit of full platform vestibules to protect the motorman from the elements. (R.J.Harley Coll.)

ROUTE BOARD

CANNON

18

TRACK GAUGE 3'6"

0 1 2 3 4 5 6
SCALE FEET

56. The water car was constructed by Mountain and Gibson of Bury and it was equipped with the same firm's 5ft. 6ins. wheelbase, Maguire type truck. It must have been an awesome sight lumbering along with brushes revolving and water spraying in all directions! (R.Cook Coll.)

57. The memory of Maidstone's trams lingers on at the Dover Transport Museum where 1:16 scale models, built by Ron Leach, depict a way of life of days gone by. (R.J.Harley)

# 5. Overhead

58. A very rare photo taken from the top deck of a tram waiting at a passing loop on the Tonbridge Road; note that the lens of the camera has foreshortened the line of traction standards. On this section of route the wiring had to be placed as near as possible over the centre line of the track to cope with fixed head trolleys which possessed limited lateral movement. Note also the white band on the traction standards which indicated a tram stop. (R.Rosa Coll.)

# 6. Finale

59. Trolleybus 26 first took to the streets of Maidstone in 1930. This vehicle has very much the appearance of a trackless tram. It is on the new service to Sutton Road which was not previously covered by its rail-bound predecessors. (H.A.Whitcombe)

# CHATHAM TRAMWAYS

## CONTENTS PART 2

## GEOGRAPHICAL SETTING

The River Medway divides Rochester from Strood as it flows towards the Thames Estuary through the Medway Gap in the North Downs. Away from the river the terrain is hilly and many of the roads in Chatham and Gillingham traverse steep gradients. Urban development is widespread, but the surrounding countryside of fields, orchards, woodlands and hop gardens is still easily accessible.

## INTRODUCTION AND ACKNOWLEDGEMENTS

Visitors to Rochester, who nowadays wander along the beautifully restored High Street, probably have no inkling that this thoroughfare once boasted a busy tramway route, part of the thriving system which linked the Medway Towns and extended right out to Rainham. Although the impact of the local tramways may have lacked the gravitas of other historical events, nevertheless in the lives of many ordinary folk, the journey to work or the pleasure outing by tram was an important part of the daily round. The reassembling of the past for this album has been made possible by the assistance of R.Cook, D.C.Padgham and R.Rosa, and I am very grateful to these gentlemen for lending me most of the views which appear in the following pages. My special thanks also go to J.H.Price and the staff of the library of the National Tramway Museum.

## HISTORICAL BACKGROUND

Rochester stands on the right bank of the Medway at a point where the ancient Watling Street crosses the river. Settlements date from Roman times and with the coming of Christianity, the town assumed a spiritual as well as a strategic significance. In 604 St. Augustine founded a bishopric here and later the Normans built a castle and a cathedral which both stand to this day. In more recent times the area has been wonderfully portrayed by Charles Dickens in Pickwick Papers and Great Expectations. Rochester's neighbour to the east is the former naval port of Chatham which, during the reign of Charles II, was the foremost naval establishment in the land. The Royal Dockyard which once covered some 500 acres with a water frontage to the Medway of nearly three miles, has now been closed, and parts have been restored as a working museum. The nineteenth century building boom in Rochester and Chatham, plus the adjacent borough of Gillingham, was accelerated by the completion of the railway from London to Strood in 1849 and the line from Chatham to Faversham, which opened in 1858.

An electric tramway scheme was suggested in 1897 as a modern means of uniting the three towns. The actual construction started by the Chatham & District Light Railways Company in March 1900 and lines situated in Chatham and Gillingham were inaugurated on 17th June 1902. The original services were:

Luton - Chatham Town Hall - Dockyard
Cemetery - Town Hall - Gillingham - Victoria Bridge(Gillingham Station)
Town Hall - Chatham Hill - Gillingham - James Street - Pier Road
Chatham Station - Town Hall - Dockyard

Operation commenced with 25 trams housed at the new depot in Luton; further vehicles were ordered as the network expanded to include new lines in Rochester opened in 1904-8. These were built by the City of Rochester and leased to the company. A reserved track to the village of Rainham was opened by the company in 1906. In the midst of this expansion, the track along Pier Road from Shalders Arms to the Bathing Pool at the Strand, Gillingham was abandoned in 1905 due to lack of passengers. By 1908 the following services were in operation ( details of the coloured route plate carried on the dash of each car are given in brackets):

Luton - Town Hall - Dockyard
    (L - D black letters on yellow backgound)

→

Frindsbury - Rochester - Town Hall -
Brompton - Gillingham Green
    (FRINDSBURY AND GILLINGHAM
    white letters on green)

Strood Hill - Rochester - Town Hall -
Brompton - Gillingham Green
    (STROOD AND GILLINGHAM  red
    letters on white)

Borstal - Delce - Rochester - Town Hall -
Brompton - Gillingham, Victoria Bridge
    (BORSTAL AND GILLINGHAM
    white letters on black)

Town Hall - Chatham Hill - Canterbury
Street - Gillingham, Shalders Arms
    (TH - G  white letters on red)

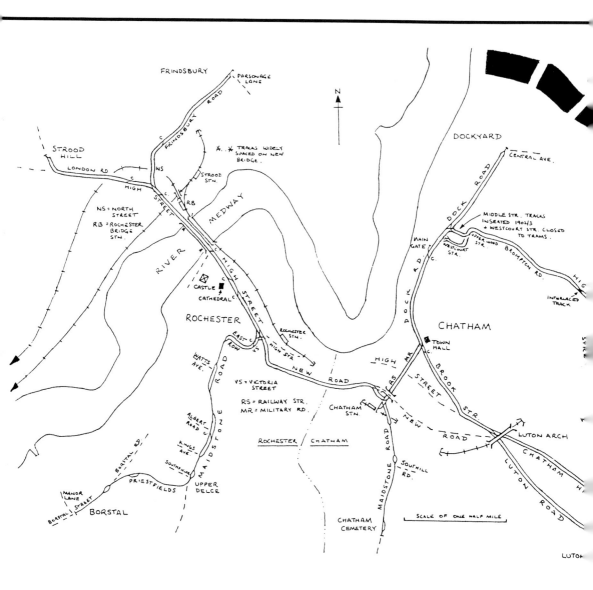

Chatham Cemetery - Town Hall - Brompton
- Gillingham, Victoria Bridge
    (C - B   white letters on purple)

Town Hall - Chatham Hill - Jezreels -
Rainham Mark - Rainham High Street
    (RAINHAM AND TOWN HALL   green
    letters on white)

Chatham Station - Town Hall - Brompton
    (S - B   white letters on brown)

Heavy traffic was carried throughout the First World War and into the 1920s. However, the need for extensive track renewals and the threat from motor bus competition created an environment where tramway survival was unlikely. The fate of the company was sealed when it was sold to Maidstone and District Motor Services in 1927; for a short period some improvements were effected, cars were repainted and the Rainham terminus improved. The end was not long in coming and all routes were abandoned on 30th September 1930 in favour of buses. Most cars were driven out to the reserved track section and there they were scrapped, an inglorious demise of a fine local transport system.

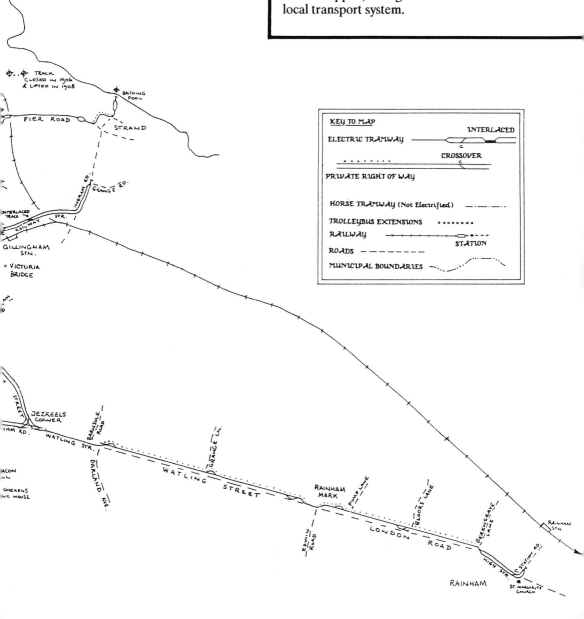

60. Our nostalgic jaunt continues further northwards at the Borstal terminus of the Chatham and District Light Railways Company. The village is probably better known for lending its name to a type of penal institution for juvenile offenders. In complete contrast to thoughts of crime and punishment, the midday

sun catches car 24 after it has arrived at the end of the line. The crew stand proudly and the conductor has one job left, to tie up the trailing trolley rope and alter the top deck indicator blind for the return to Gillingham. (R.J.Harley Coll.)

61. A car descends Star Hill, Rochester passing a line of traction poles which display the distinctive finials and bases demanded by the City fathers to enhance the image of the local tramways. One gets the impression that Rochester was never entirely happy sharing its transport system with its less salubrious neighbours, Chatham and Gillingham. (R.Rosa Coll.)

63. Several local postcard publishers celebrated the arrival of electric traction in High Street, Rochester by publishing scenes of this latest public transport marvel. It is easy to forget how the trams, with their frequent services and cheap fares, broadened the horizons of working folk. They enabled people to live further from their place of work and to escape from the daily toil by travelling into the countryside out of the stale air of the city. (J.H.Price Coll.)

62. At the foot of Star Hill in the 1920s, cloche hats are all the fashion as the driver takes his eyes off the road to check his footwear. (H.A.Whitcombe)

64. A Frindsbury to Gillingham car edges past the pomp and circumstance going on in the High Street. A lady on the top deck speaks to the lad in front; the onlookers on pavement level have plenty of time to stand and stare. (R.Cook Coll.)

65. Except for the trams, not much has changed along here since the time of Charles Dickens, who wrote with some affection of the buildings and way of life in nineteenth century Rochester. The clock outside the old Corn Exchange shows 10:05 am. The narrow High Street is suffering a dose of traffic congestion as a Gillingham bound car waits for an obstructing cart to clear the tramlines. (R.J.Harley Coll.)

66. Out of the shadows we look in the direction of the bridge over the Medway. The heavier wires coming from the standard on the right, are the cables feeding traction current to the overhead. (R.Rosa Coll.)

THE FIRST TRAM THROUGH ROCHESTER

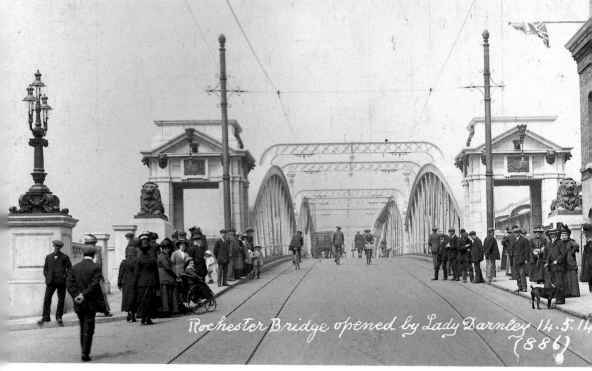

*Rochester Bridge opened by Lady Darnley 14.5.14*
*(886)*

67. The date is April 1908 and a test car makes cautious progress over the new lines in Rochester. The motorman is about to bring his charge onto the bridge. (R.Rosa Coll.)

Extract from Borough of Chatham Bye-Laws and Regulations of 1899.

The driver of every car shall maintain a sufficient distance between his own and the next car.

68. The pedigree of Rochester Bridge stretches back into the mists of time. After earlier Roman and medieval structures had perished, a more solid stone edifice arose in 1387-92. It was demolished in 1856 to be replaced by a new iron bridge which in turn was reconstructed in 1914. The opening ceremony by Lady Darnley was an occasion when tramway officials could look with pride on the new trackwork set to the side of the carriageway. On the new river crossing the opportunity was also taken to dispense with poles and attach the overhead wires directly to the bridge girders. (J.H.Price Coll.)

69. On the other bank of the river we encounter car 16 in Strood High Street. To the right of the tram is the original Rochester Bridge station, later a victim of "rationalisation" in July 1917, when it was closed for good. The railways in this area are covered fully in companion Middleton Press volumes: *Dartford to Sittingbourne* and *Bromley South to Rochester*. (R.J.Harley Coll.)

70. We now meet up with car 5 once more, this time on the return trip back to base in Chatham. Its proving run continues and the "test pilot" motorman halts here in Strood for this episode in locomotion history to be recorded. (R.Rosa Coll.)

72. The tram in the picture has just begun its journey to Gillingham and is obviously not in much of a hurry as it is being overtaken by a cyclist. (R.Rosa Coll.)

71. Water, water everywhere...! There is obviously some speculation as to whether the tram will make it or not. From the look of the stalled vehicle under the railway bridge, it seems unlikely that the tram will be able to slip through without its electrics and motors suffering. (R.Rosa Coll.)

73. We now direct our glance eastwards to
New Road, Rochester where car 40 is very
close to the boundary with Chatham. The tram
is on the short lived service, Delce Grange to
Gillingham Green (1906-8).
(R.J.Harley Coll.)

No indecent or seditious advertisements shall
be placed upon any car.

# 8. Chatham Cemetery to Town Hall

74. We cross into Chatham proper to witness car 23 by Chatham Cemetery. The C - B letters on the dash indicate that the tram was operating to Gillingham, Victoria Bridge. The coloured background of the indicator sign, in this case purple, would be a help to intending passengers who were illiterate. (R.Rosa Coll.)

75. A 1920s view of car 8 at the terminus. We assume the conductor on the top deck was not about to submit to some unseen gunman and hand over the day's takings, but more likely, he was trying to grab the trolley pole for a quick turn round. (H.A.Whitcombe)

76. Where Maidstone Road joins Ordnance Street, the spur from Chatham station comes in from the right. On the extreme left of the picture is the statue to Thomas Waghorn (1800-50), a native of Chatham, who pioneered the overland route to India in 1829. (R.Rosa Coll.)

Maidstone Rd station app[roach] & Waghorn memorial, Chatham (807)

77.  Out from under the viaduct emerges a Chatham tramcar. The bridge, which was totally rebuilt in 1902 to allow the trams to pass underneath, carries New Road over Railway Street. Tracks were authorised on the viaduct, however, the novel spectacle of a tramway flyover never materialised.  (J.H.Price Coll.)

78.  Before descending Railway Street on the way to Chatham Town Hall, we pause with the photographer on the viaduct, to look down at a tram on service S-B nearing journey's end; it is being pursued by the works car.
(R.Rosa Coll.)

Pier

Holborn
Wharf

t's Wharf

Trav. Cr.

Scott's
Medway St.
Wharf

110

80

Schools

D.Fn.

The Shrubbery

Town
Hall

72

P.H.

TRAMWAY

P.H.

MEDWAY STREET

Music
Hall

P.H.

P.H.

HOLBORN LANE

GLOBE LANE

MILITARY ROAD

Club

P.H.

P.H.

Club

VATE'S PLACE

P.H.

Club

Club

NELSON ROAD

GEORGE STREET

P.H.

Bank

P.H.

Theatre

Bank

P.H.

Bank

LB

Chap.

AVONDALE ST.

Club

FAIR

R. SOLOMON RD.

ST GEORGE'S SQ.

Bk.

Bk.

P.H.

P.H.

Masonic
Hall

Saw Mills

P.O.

HIGH STREET

Hotel

CAMBRIDGE TER.

P.H.

Printing
Works

ROAD

Timber Yards

St. John's
Church

THE PADDOCK

FULLAGERS YARD

Hotel

MEETING HOUSE LANE

L.B.

16

Congl.
Hall

P.H.

Sun. Sch.

Police Station

St. John's
Rectory

St. Mary's
Rectory

L.B.

Congl.
Ch.

Waghorn
Memorial

CLOVER STREET

RICH

Naval Ch.
Institute

P.H.

TRAMWAY

L.B.

Sm.

Church

79. Further down the hill in Military Road, car
30 passes Chatham post office.
(R.J.Harley Coll.)

When any carriage contains the full licensed
number of passengers a conspicuous notice to that
effect shall be placed on the carriage, and no
additional person shall enter, mount or remain on any
such carriage when warned by the conductor not to
do so.

80. Finally we arrive at the imposing Town Hall which was completed in January 1900. This postcard was posted in March 1905 and it depicts car 9 outside the Eagle Tavern. It is evident that there was no finer place to view the town on a summer's day than from the top of a tramcar. (R.Rosa Coll.)

81. Three window car 31 with the route board above the fleet number heads for Chatham Cemetery. In the opposite direction, four window car 9 with its route board in a slightly different location, tarries a while.
(R.J.Harley Coll.)

82. At the Town Hall junction, car 4 halts at the terminus in readiness for the return trip to Rainham. The driver has slung his coat over the stairway handrails and the key on the controller seems already in place for an imminent departure. (C.F.Klapper. Omnibus Society)

83. Everyone boarding the car in the background wants a top deck seat to enjoy the fine weather. One chap is waving in the direction of the photographer, whilst a Rochester bound car prepares to tackle the hill. (K.H.Rudolph)

84. A last look from Military Road sees car 17 loading passengers for the trip to Gillingham, Victoria Bridge. (R.Rosa Coll.)

85. Flags and bunting decorate the Town Hall in celebration of Chatham Navy Week, when the maritime traditions of the borough came to the fore and local inhabitants had the chance to inspect the Senior Service. The postcard publisher obviously had plenty of stocks of this view since it was still on sale in 1949, almost twenty years after the passing of the trams! (A.J.Watkins Coll.)

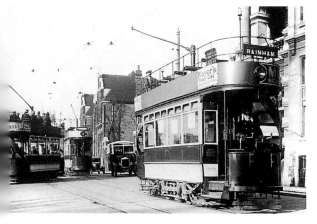

86. Three trams in sight with a guest appearance from the Snodland bus. Already motor traffic is on the increase and competition for road space will soon become critical for the rail-bound tramcars. (H.A.Whitcombe)

87. Summer 1902 and the tram has the highway to itself. Two ladies on the top deck seem to be having some trouble finding their way down, perhaps they were still unfamiliar with the new mode of transport. All passengers were expected to alight and descend at the conductor's end of the car.
(A.J.Watkins Coll.)

88. The lower saloon is furnished with Edwardian trimmings; the curtains at the windows and the fancy glass ventilator top lights symbolise an age when public service vehicles were a matter of local pride.
(R.Rosa Coll.)

CHATHAM & DISTRICT LIGHT RAILWAYS CO

# 9. Luton Arch to Depot

89. Car 5 sways over the junction of the lines from Brook Street to Luton Road. Luton Arch in the background carries the main railway line from Chatham to Gillingham. (R.J.Harley Coll.)

90. The photographer has positioned himself in the middle of the tramlines on Chatham Hill and will shortly have to vacate the spot to allow passage of car 42 on the Town Hall to Gillingham via Canterbury Street service. (R.Rosa Coll.)

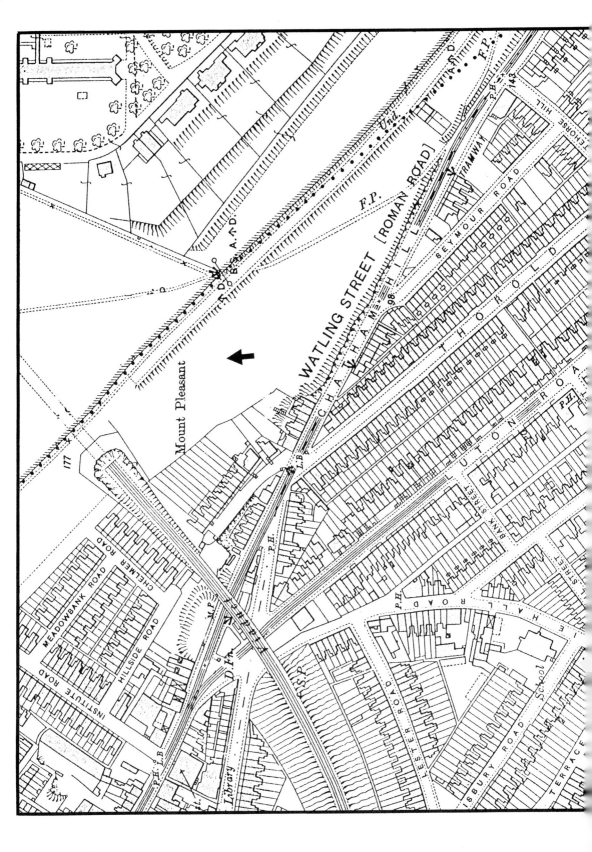

91. We arrive at the depot seen here shortly before the opening. The car sheds are to the left of the picture, they had a capacity of fifty cars. On the right is the gable end of the boiler house, next to this is the generating house with the lean-to roof of the narrow office building attached. (Tramway and Railway World)

92. Car 1 waits over one of the inspection pits at Luton depot; the empty road next to the tram is a reminder that the rest of the fleet was out on revenue service. (J.H.Price Coll.)

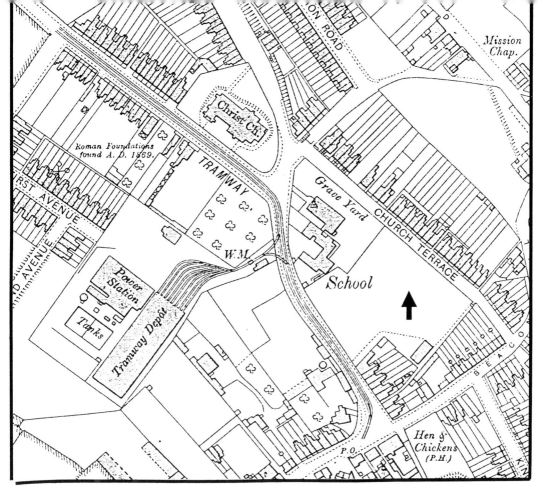

93. Relegated to works duties, car 16 lurks at the back of the depot; it is coupled to a permanent way trolley. Note the double bulkhead doors at the entrance to the lower saloon. (P.W.Boulding)

94. Another interior depot view with a side view of works car 19 which shows the timber boarding of the bodywork. (R.Cook Coll.)

95. Before leaving the depot we glance at the generating equipment needed to supply electricity for the tramway. The three principal engines were of the horizontal compound type, each developing 480 HP when working at 100 revs. per minute. Each engine was connected to a 200 KW electric generator.
(Tramway and Railway World)

96. The terminus of the route was by the Hen and Chickens. An unidentified car from the 26-35 series bears the destination board DOCKYARD which is our next port of call. (R.Rosa Coll.)

97. At the corner of Dock Road everything seems under control as a tram starts the ascent of Westcourt Street. Tragically, death and destruction were visited on this site on 30th October 1902 when car 19 got out of control on the hill and overturned here at the points killing four people and injuring over fifty. The track in Westcourt Street was ordered to be closed by Major Pringle, the Board of Trade inspecting officer. An avoiding line via Middle Street was later constructed as an alternative to Westcourt Street. (A.J.Watkins Coll.)

98. The dockyard boundary wall seems to have had a fatal attraction for Chatham tramcars in the company's early years. Luckily, this time on 15th July 1908 the tram, which ran away down Middle Street, remained upright. The only injuries were minor ones to driver and conductor. Some superstitious crews later lobbied unsuccessfully to have the terminus redesignated Maidstone Road instead of Chatham Cemetery! (R.Cook Coll.)

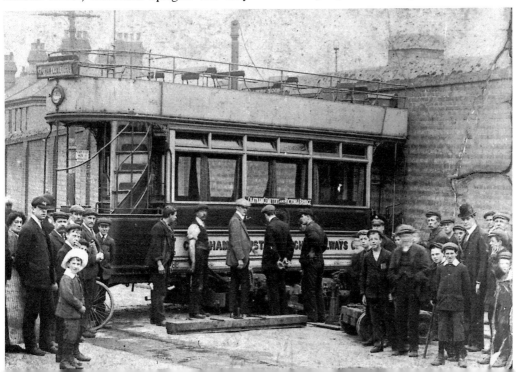

99. The day's work is over and the reliable, efficient tramcars await the crowds of homeward bound workers. In their heyday trams were responsible for transporting large numbers of people in cities and towns all over Great Britain. (R.J.Harley Coll.)

Every driver of a car on coming in sight of a vehicle standing or travelling on any part of the road so as not to leave sufficient space for the car to pass shall sound his bell or whistle as a warning to the person in charge of such vehicle, and that person shall with reasonable dispatch cause such vehicle to be removed so as not to obstruct the car, and every such driver shall sound his bell or whistle at the corner of any street.

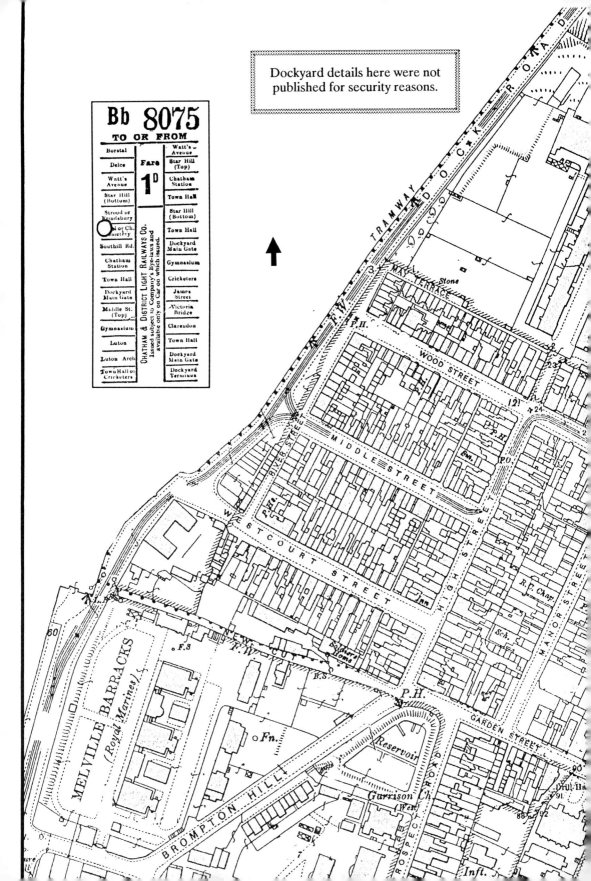

Dockyard details here were not published for security reasons.

**Bb 8075**
TO OR FROM

| | | |
|---|---|---|
| Borstal | | Watt's Avenue |
| Delce | **Fare** | Star Hill (Top) |
| Watt's Avenue | **1ᴰ** | Chatham Station |
| Star Hill (Bottom) | | Town Hall |
| Strood or Frindsbury | | Star Hill (Bottom) |
| St or Ch. Cemetry | | Town Hall |
| Southill Rd. | | Dockyard Main Gate |
| Chatham Station | | Gymnasium |
| Town Hall | | Cricketers |
| Dockyard Main Gate | | James Street |
| Middle St. (Top) | | Victoria Bridge |
| Gymnasium | | Clarendon |
| Luton | | Town Hall |
| Luton Arch | | Dockyard Main Gate |
| Town Hall or Cricketers | | Dockyard Terminus |

CHATHAM & DISTRICT LIGHT RAILWAYS Co. Issued subject to Company's Bye-laws and available only on Car on which issued

100. A sailor from the nearby base strolls nonchalantly towards the camera one fine day in Gillingham High Street. The lines to the left serve Canterbury Street and the approaching tram will proceed straight along the High Street to the Victoria Bridge terminus. (R.Rosa Coll.)

101. The policeman standing by the centre traffic island surveys the scene as a Strood bound tram clatters over the points of the triangular junction. (R.Rosa Coll.)

High Street and Bank, Gillingham

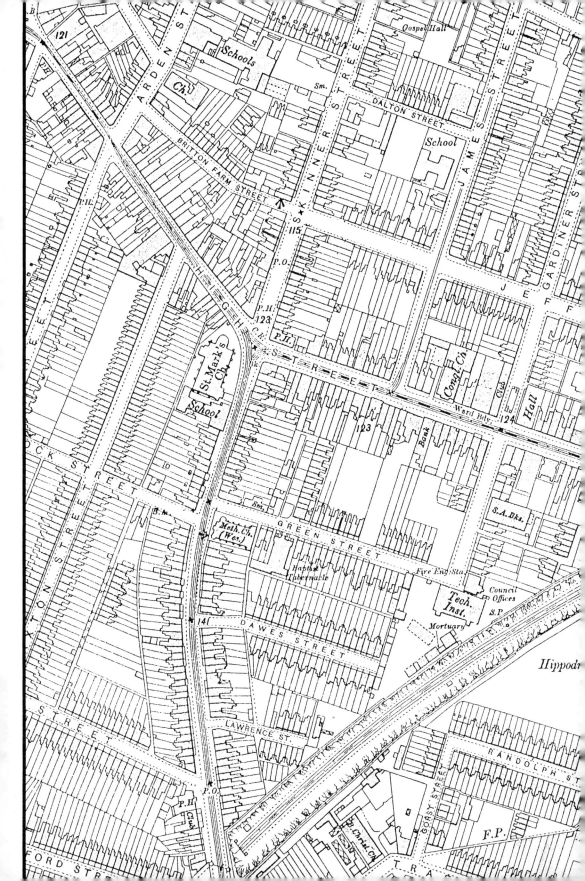

102. Car 8 halts by the stop sign before veering to the driver's left past the bank into Canterbury Street. This tram had already made the sharp turn from James Street to High Street about where the cart is parked on the left hand side of the road.   (R.Rosa Coll.)

103. We continue round the corner to observe car 46 loading in Canterbury Street. The Maidstone and District bus timetable fixed to the lamp standard in the centre of the picture, is a portent of doom for the Chatham trams. (D.C.Padgham Coll.)

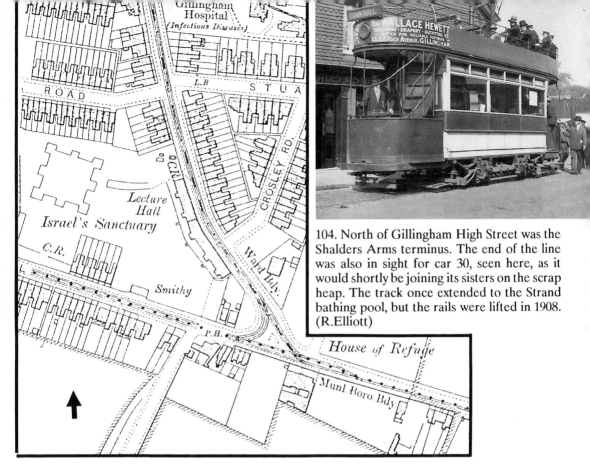

104. North of Gillingham High Street was the Shalders Arms terminus. The end of the line was also in sight for car 30, seen here, as it would shortly be joining its sisters on the scrap heap. The track once extended to the Strand bathing pool, but the rails were lifted in 1908. (R.Elliott)

105. We are looking along the ancient thoroughfare of Watling Street where it joins Canterbury Street at Jezreels Corner. Two company employees are engaged in cleaning out the pointwork; in the distance a car on the Rainham route approaches. (R.Rosa Coll.)

# 11. Across the fields to Rainham

106. A bold initiative of the company was the planning and construction of the Rainham extension. The track was placed on private right of way alongside what was later to become the A2. Car 8 demonstrates the virtues of a route segregated from the other traffic; unfortunately just behind the tram, a detour had to be made at Rainham Mark back onto the main road. (A.W.Bates)

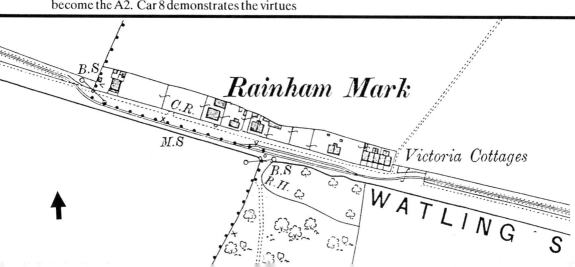

107. After crossing Pump Lane a cutting took
the line across country to avoid the gradient of
the neighbouring London Road.
(Tramway and Railway World)

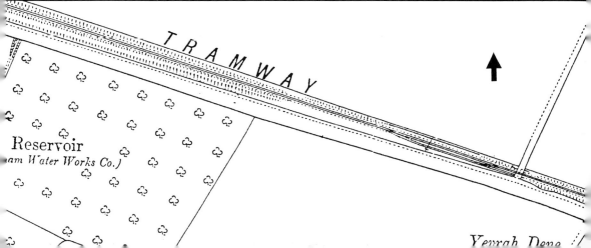

TRAMWAY

Reservoir
am Water Works Co.)

Yevrah Dene

108. Cattle grids and railings guard the entrance to Bloors Lane where a tramway siding was conveniently installed next to the passing loop. (Tramway and Railway World)

109. A crowd gathers round car 32 at the end of its run from Chatham Town Hall. The conductor is just coming round with the pole and in a few seconds he will place the trolley wheel on the overhead wire. (R.J.Harley Coll.)

110. This was where the trams finished in Rainham in front of St.Margaret's Church parts of which date from the thirteenth century. The

Rainham to Strood Hill service was started in 1928 and gave a total ride of around eight miles. (R.J.Harley Coll.)

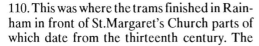

Tram Terminus, Rainham.

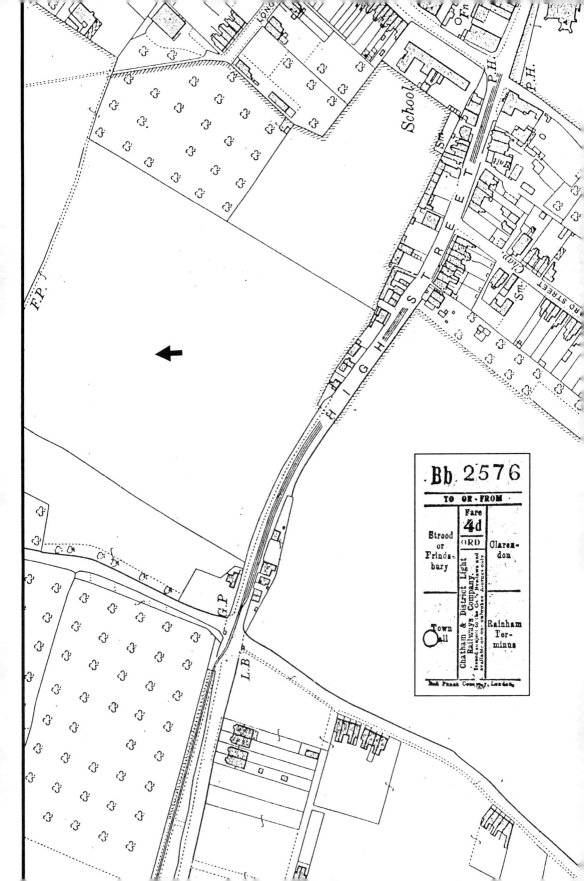

LONG

School

P.H.

P.H.

Sm

STREET

O

HIGH STREET

RD STREET

Sm

F.P.

G.P.

L.B.

Bb. 2576

TO OR·FROM

| | Fare | |
|---|---|---|
| Strood or Frinds-bury | **4d** ORD | Clarendon |
| Town Hall | Chatham & District Light Railways Company. Issued subject to the Co's. Bye-laws and available on one unbroken journey only | Rainham Ter-minus |

Bell Punch Company, London.

111. All ready for the off, motorman and conductor pose stiffly as they stand on opposite sides of their vehicle. The next trams to be encountered along this road would be the cars of the Isle of Thanet Tramways at Westbrook, or the Dover Corporation system at River; both undertakings are described in other Middleton Press albums. In 1929 the tracks were extended round the corner into Station Road so that trams could stand away from the through traffic. (R.J.Harley Coll.)

112. Here at the final Rainham terminus we end our tramway tour of the Medway Towns. Shortly after this photo was taken, the trams vanished for good, the rails were lifted and life became firmly attuned to the internal combustion engine. (R.J.Harley Coll.)

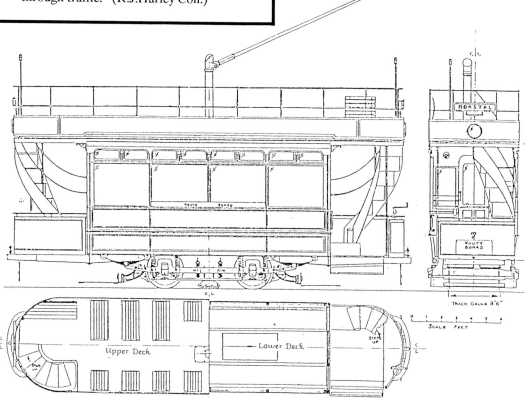

# 12. Rolling Stock

All trams were of the traditional British open top variety; each car was equipped with a four wheel, two motored truck of 6ft. wheelbase. The track gauge was 3ft 6ins. The Chatham livery until around 1927 was light grass green with ivory window surrounds and rocker panels. The green areas were lined in gold and the ivory parts were lined in green; the title of the undertaking appeared in gold letters on the rocker panel until about 1921. A new manager, A.J.Bousfield, was appointed in 1927 and the colour scheme was simplified. Cars were repainted in an unlined plain green and ivory livery, with the fleet number on the dash appearing in a dull yellow instead of the former gold shaded blue.

**CARS 1-25.** Built by George Milnes & Co. in 1901 and supplied in 1902, these cars had reversed stairs and seated 24 inside and 28 outside. Cars 1-15 were fitted with a single bulkhead door at each end of the lower saloon, whereas cars 16-25 possessed twin sliding bulkhead doors. The headlamp was located on the canopy above the driver and this feature was common to all Chatham trams bar the second hand car 52 from Maidstone. Car 19 was an accident victim in 1902 and was retired permanently; car 19's truck, which was a standard 6ft. Brill 21E, and electrical gear were then used under the works car.

**CARS 26-35.** These were Brush built cars supplied in 1903. Unlike the first batch of trams, they had three window lower saloons and half turn spiral stairs. They rode on Brush A type 6ft. wheelbase trucks. They had seats for 22 on the lower deck and 26 on top.

**CAR 36.** This tram was delivered in 1903 as a replacement for car 19; in all respects it was similar to the 16-25 series.

**CARS 37-48.** These were constructed by Brush of Loughborough and were delivered in two batches: cars 37-46 in 1907, cars 47 & 48 in 1911. They had four window lower saloons which seated 22 people; the upper deck accommodated 26 and was reached by the usual half turn spiral staircases. They were mounted on Brush Aa 6ft. wheelbase trucks.

**CARS 49-51.** Supplied by the UEC at Preston, these cars were assembled in the depot in 1911. They were slightly larger cars than the Chatham norm and they seated 24 inside and 26 outside. Each car weighed 13 tons, which meant that these trams were some of the heaviest of their type in Great Britain to operate on the narrow gauge.

**CAR 52.** This car was acquired from Maidstone Corporation where it bore the fleet number 14. It entered service in 1928, but was prone to derailments. The situation was remedied when the wheels were reprofiled to suit Chatham requirements, the car then saw out its remaining days on the Rainham route.

**WORKS CAR 19.** This maid of all work was constructed in 1903 partly from the remains of the ill-fated car 19. Evidently the Chatham staff were not superstitious as this fleet number was subsequently applied to the works car! As can be seen from photographs, it had a rather home made appearance with box like bodywork and open driver's platforms at each end.

113. A tram from the first series of cars to be delivered; it is seen here late in its career. (H.A.Whitcombe)

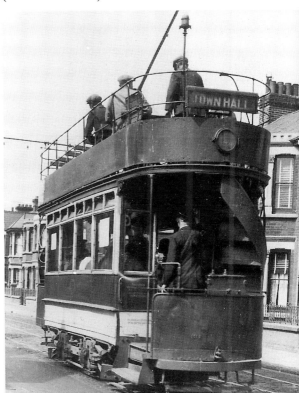

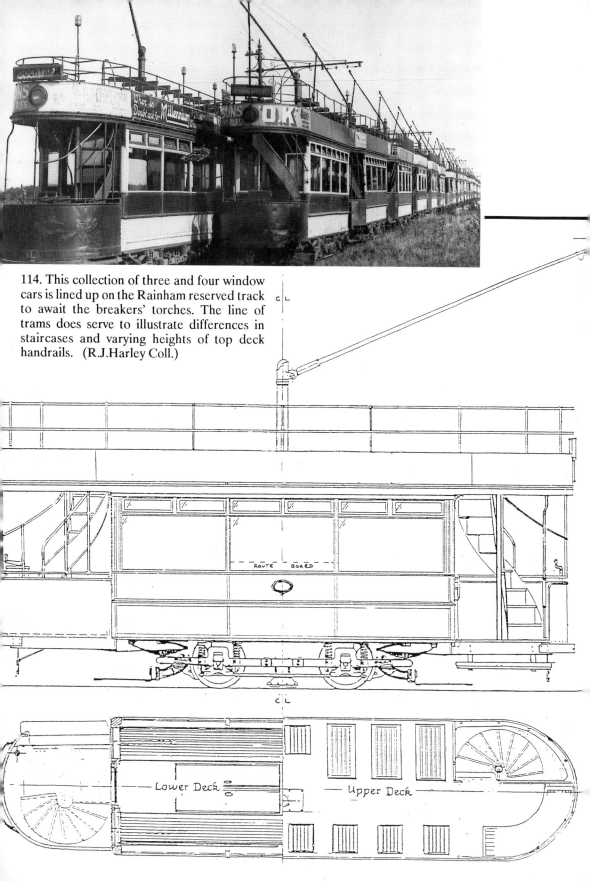

114. This collection of three and four window cars is lined up on the Rainham reserved track to await the breakers' torches. The line of trams does serve to illustrate differences in staircases and varying heights of top deck handrails. (R.J.Harley Coll.)

ROUTE BOARD

C L

Lower Deck — Upper Deck

115. Car 51 was the last vehicle to be delivered new to the Chatham tramways. (H.A.Whitcombe)

116. The small ex-Maidstone car 52 is seen here in its last days; apart from a change of livery, its new owners have made no significant alterations. (D.C.Padgham Coll.)

117. The works car has been variously described as a garden shed on wheels or a mobile beach hut! Well, you can made up your own mind, one thing is certain, it performed a very useful function in the day-to-day running of the system. (R.Cook Coll.)

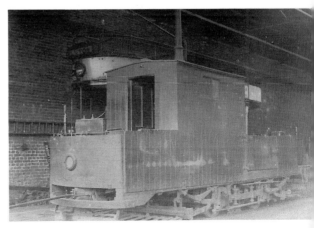

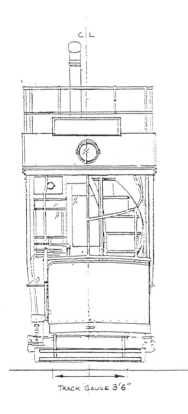

C L

TRACK GAUGE 3'6"

0 1 2 3 4 5 6
SCALE FEET

CHATHAM CARS 26-35

118. A rare photo of one of the trams from the 26-35 series in festive mood. The decorations, the greenery and the coloured lights were in honour of the Chatham carnival of 1903, when this car would have taken part in the procession. It would also have toured the routes at night, a splendid sight with all the different light bulbs brightly illuminated. (D.C.Padgham Coll.)

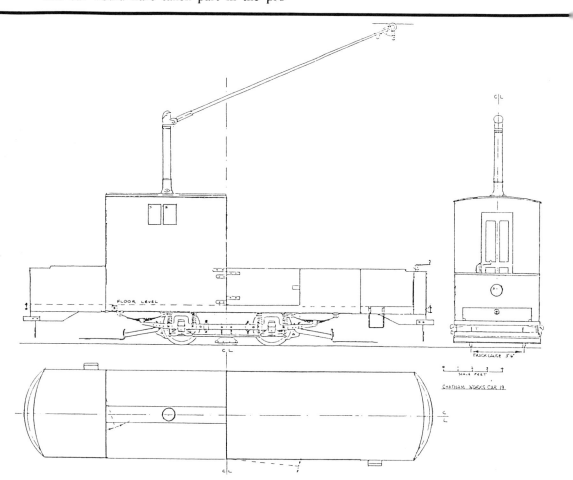

FLOOR LEVEL

C/L

C L

TRACK GAUGE 3'6"

SCALE FEET

CHATHAM WORKS CAR 19

C/L

C/L

# 13. Finale

119. The end is not far away and concern about the future is mirrored on the faces of the tram crews. Some would find employment with the replacing buses, but others would be cast aside with bleak prospects of finding another job. (A.J.Watkins Coll.)

120. Tramlines still exist in Chatham, albeit in the former naval dockyard which was equipped with grooved rails for standard gauge railway wagons. About 80 acres is now occupied by the Chatham Historical Dockyard and the tracks could be used for historic tramcars to assist the public around the vast site. Although not actually used in the dockyard, they did bring workers to the gates. Other views are in pictures 89-95 in the Middleton Press album *Dartford to Sittingbourne*. (V.Mitchell)